GW00362954

MAN HANDLING

Deborah McKinlay

HEADLINE

For Tex

First published in 1997
by HEADLINE BOOK PUBLISHING
10 9 8 7 6 5 4 3 2 1

British Library Cataloguing in Publication Data
McKinlay, Deborah
Man handling
1. Man-woman relationships – Humour
I. Title 306.7'0207

ISBN 0 7472 2068 9

Designed by Isobel Gillan
Printed and bound in Great Britain by Mackays of Chatham PLC

HEADLINE BOOK PUBLISHING
A division of Hodder Headline PLC, 338 Euston Road, London, NW1 3BH

When it comes to dealing with women, men have their fair share of strategies. However, most men just pick out one or two of these and stick to them throughout their adult lives. (A man tends to follow this same policy with regard to sports teams, haircuts and shoe styles.) A woman is a rather more fickle creature. A woman is a great believer in strategies. If one is unsuccessful, she likes to give another one a try. (A policy she is particularly partial to where haircuts are concerned.) Sometimes a man hasn't had a chance to draw breath in the time it takes for this to happen.

acting cool

And then what did he say?

In the early days of a romantic relationship, a woman is often rather more in the dark than she'd like to be. This situation is exacerbated if a man says anything like 'I'll call you'. A woman believes that asking a man to be more specific with regard to a pronouncement of this type would probably cause him to react negatively. (A woman is not usually way off the mark in this belief.) So she tries very hard not to. She tries very hard too, when the man does call, not to ask when he'll call again. A woman believes that a casual approach will encourage the man to *keep* calling. (A woman is usually bang on the button in this belief.)

He said he'd call me.

Oh well, never mind.

Often, a woman finds maintaining her little-bit-distant façade a strain because there are lots of things she'd like to know. Still, she doesn't want to go and blow it by saying something silly like 'Am I going to get my heart broken?' to a man who is very clearly in let's-see-how-it-goes mode. The woman behaves in as relaxed a manner as she can manage whenever she is dealing with the man and looks elsewhere for comfort and clues as to the future of the relationship.

Some of the things women look to for comfort and clues as to the future of a relationship

- Their friends
- Complete strangers

getting some advice from the other girls

ASK AUNT LOLA
ADVICE FOR THE
LOVELORN

Dear Aunt Lola

I am thirty-two years old and I have a good job and great friends, but I get very depressed sometimes because I think I might never meet a man and have a family. Is this normal?

Do you feel guilty when you eat desserts?

Have you ever bought something because the packaging matched your bathroom?

Are you a woman?

A. L

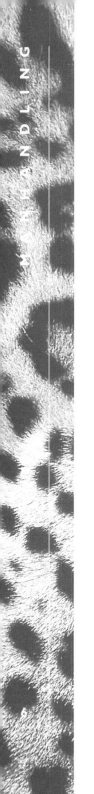

Some of the other things women look to for comfort and clues as to the future of a relationship

- Astrology
- Numerology
- Pink rose quartz love crystals
- The ancient Asian art of furniture placement
- The ancient Asian art of I Ching
- The tarot line
- A palm reader
- A psychic
- A programme on the telly about handwriting analysis
- This thing where you write down everything that you're looking for in a man and you shout it out at the full moon

Most women would think that a man who did this stuff was a bit of a crackpot. Most women would think that a woman who did this stuff and took it *really* seriously was a bit of a crackpot.

Telephone companies everywhere are grateful to all the women who've paid fifty pence per minute for a bit of fun.

Mostly, a man doesn't know the half of what goes on with regard to the beyond-life-as-we-know-it experiences of a woman, but he quite likes it when she reads his stars out to him.

When a man does keep calling, a woman finds it easier to maintain her little-bit-distantness.

not being too available

Still, she is not absolutely certain that this will do the trick with regard to the *keeping* calling and the future-prospects-of-her-heart problem. She figures a wee bit more effort is called for. She makes this effort after she has told the man she is free on Friday.

Things a woman has done because she is going out with a man she fancies on Friday

We'll take a cab because you probably don't want to walk very far in those shoes, and by the way, your hair looks fabulous.

- ■ Thought about outfits
- ■ Talked about outfits with a friend
- ■ Bought an outfit
- ■ Bought a bra
- ■ Had a haircut
- ■ Painted her fingernails
- ■ Painted her toenails
- ■ Tidied up her flat

- Gone on a sunbed

He's a gigolo.

- Not gone on a sunbed because her friend told her they give you cancer; bought some stuff that makes you look like you've gone on a sunbed instead
- Removed the vast amounts of hair that have accumulated on her body during the weeks/months/years when men she fancies have been thin on the ground
- Paid someone to remove the vast amounts of hair
- Booked a facial
- Cancelled the facial because her friend told her they give you spots
- Panicked because she thought she was getting a spot
- Bought some stuff for spots and exceeded the stated dose
- Bought something French for ridding thighs of cellulite
- Had her hopes dashed when she read on the label that the cellulite-ridding stuff takes three weeks to work
- Developed a steely will with regard to mid-morning ham-and-cheese croissants
- Bought a lipstick which will have to be removed with paint stripper three days after it is applied
- Bought body lotion with a nice smell
- Left work early and hurried home with the nice-smelling body lotion in order to have a lovely long bath

He's gay.

- Had a lovely long bath
- Exfoliated her elbows and knees
- Almost choked herself doing that thing where you spray the perfume in the air and walk through it
- Worried a bit at the last minute in case it looks as though she's gone to a lot of effort

He's French.

Men should note that women do all these things when they're going on holiday with another woman.

taking an interest in his hobbies

A woman finds that all her efforts pay off, up to a point. It's this point:

- The man has chipped persistently at the woman's little-bit-distantness
- He has *kept* calling
- He has shown appreciation with regard to the pre-Friday-night efforts
- He has done everything he can to convince the woman that her heart is in safe hands, and, often, that *his* heart is in hers

- The woman drops her façade
- The man becomes a little bit distant

Women often think that a relationship will be on a much firmer footing once it becomes physical.

Women do not want to read a list of things they've done because they thought this.

making the first move

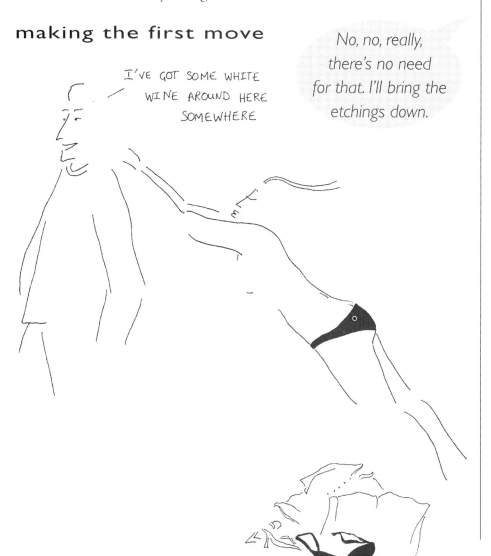

I'VE GOT SOME WHITE WINE AROUND HERE SOMEWHERE

No, no, really, there's no need for that. I'll bring the etchings down.

TAKING THE LEAD

number of players: two
ONE MALE, *cute*
ONE FEMALE, *keen*

object
MALE: to keep his options open
FEMALE: to chase him until he catches her

points scored by
MALE: for pretending it was his idea
FEMALE: for not getting all neurotic about it being her idea

catchphrases
- *So, anyway . . . I just called to say hi . . .*
- *I thought . . . if you weren't doing anything*
- *How funny, I've always wanted to go to a darts marathon*

points deducted for
MALE:
- *unnecessarily cutting snubs*
- *constant reminders at later dates that it was all her idea*
FEMALE:
- *paying no attention whatsoever to gentle rejection*
- *complete denials at later dates that she had anything to do with it*

characteristic moves
FEMALE: rehearses and plans every move she makes, often retreating
slightly after a forward step in order to pluck up the courage
required for the next one
MALE: goes along for the ride

When the man becomes a little bit distant, the woman has to come up with a New Plan.

That's all right. Women come up with New Plans all the time.

coming up with a new plan

Quite often a woman wakes up on a Thursday morning with a New Plan. The New Plan might have nothing whatsoever to do with a man, but quite often, it does.

These are some New Plans that have something to do with a man:

- I'm not going to call him (not once; not at all; I am Absolutely Definitely NOT GOING TO CALL HIM)
- I'm going to be *really* sweet to him (to make up for last week)
- I'm not going to mention―― (something that she's mentioned incessantly for about three months)

Mostly, a woman finds it hard to get right through the weekend without giving up on the New Plan.

This means that she has to come up with another New Plan on Tuesday:

- I'm going to be *really* aloof with him until he stops taking the fact that I am always *really* sweet to him for granted

Sometimes a New Plan involves a New Look.

This New Look might have something to do with a man, but it is just as likely to have something to do with a film the woman saw with Uma Thurman in it:

ASK AUNT LOLA
ADVICE FOR THE
FEISTY LOVELORN

Dear Aunt Lola

*I split up with my boyfriend three months ago. But
now I'm so lonely and my life feels so empty I'm
thinking of going back to him.*

What do you think?

Gee, no jobs, gyms, books, movie theatres, pianos,
plants, parks, actors, pets, dance schools, art galleries,
cookery classes, sports teams or other people in your
area, huh, honey?

- I'm going to get my hair cut just like Uma's (women know that a haircut just like Uma's is as potentially life-changing as anything to do with a man)

Quite often a woman gets an idea for a New Plan from a book or a magazine. There are books and magazines galore full of love-life tips. None of them are called *Men Who Love Too Much*. Anyway, the woman gleans quite a bit about the workings of the male psyche from these, and sometimes she decides to investigate further. She does some general gender research reading.

doing some general gender research reading

Categories:

- The kind which requires an **A**, **B**, or **C** response. Enormously enhanced by the presence of friends and a bottle of white wine

Right, number two . . .
If a man meets three women,
A *an entrepreneur*
B *a homemaker*
C *an academic, which one is he most likely to ask out?*

- The kind which encourages understanding. Bits get read out to men in the vague hope that this will help *them* to understand
- The man-catching kind. Hidden very far back in a bedside drawer

The one with the biggest boobs?

Things a woman knows because she has done some general gender research reading (or she might have seen it on *Oprah*)

- It is hard for men to communicate their feelings
- A man might find it easier to communicate his feelings if he is encouraged to read this book
- A man has got about two billion light years of gender preconditioning to overcome before he can operate a hoover on a regular basis
- A man is not watching the television; he is In His Cave
- A man who does not listen to his answering machine tape in front of a woman fits into Category 1 of 'Profile of a Cheat'
- A man can spot a woman who is desperate at two hundred paces
- A woman who follows these ten easy tips will not appear to be quite so desperate
- A man has more of the innate skills required for reversing into a parking space really well

It's a commitment-phobic, hooked-on-pseudo-intimacy, genetically imprinted, macho-defensiveness thing

- A woman has more of the innate skills required for reversing into a parking space moderately well and preventing the kids from killing each other at the same time
- A man who leaves the room when a woman says the word 'commit' is not Ready To Commit

No, I just don't fancy you.

Any men who are getting all puffed up about women being so fascinated with them should note that the world is not short of women who will read 'How To Make Your Own Photo Frames' with rapt attention.

Not only are some of a woman's plans not to do with a man, a lot of them are not to do with today.

forward planning

We can get a telephone engineer to your house some time on Friday 2 June 2043.

An example:
A woman says something like this to a man:

'Are we going to stop for the night on the way up to your sister's next week or do you want to drive straight through?'

and a man says something like:

'I don't know. Can't we see how we feel at the time?'

Hopeless. I'm getting married that day.

The man says this because he hates Forward Planning. As a rule, women are addicted to it.

Quite a few men (mainly bachelors) think that women's Forward Planning always has something to do with *them* (moving in/marriage/babies). They are wrong.

Most of women's Forward Planning has to do with wearing appropriate shoes. (Men who are no longer bachelors usually develop a vague inkling of this.)

Well, OK, some of a woman's Forward Planning *is* to do with a man. This situation tends to be exacerbated by Let's-see-how-it-goes mode. In circumstances like these, a woman doesn't Forward Plan exactly; what she does is while away an idle moment or two daydreaming and, maybe, have a casual sort of a chat with a friend about how it *might* go. (This chat would last around 113 minutes on average.)

When a sensible modern woman catches herself doing Forward Planning to do with a man (around minute 114), she tries very hard to stop herself.

Her friends are no help at all in this process.

17

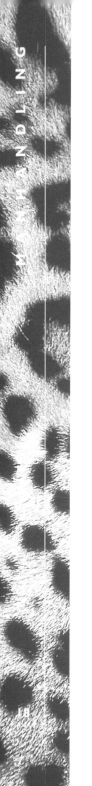

Dear Aunt Lola

I feel as though I'm just marking time dating guys who aren't The One. I can't wait to meet a man I can settle down with so I can get on and start really living.

You got it wrong, doll.

A man is the frosting.
LIFE is the cake.

A. L.

It is unlikely that a modern woman wants every relationship she has with a man to progress to the moving in/marriage/babies stage. A modern woman is perfectly capable of having fun with a fellow whom she has no desire to see wandering around her kitchen in his boxer shorts. But if a woman meets a man who looks pretty cute in his boxer shorts, a man who manages to locate the kitchen without a map, she sometimes decides that she'd really like it if he were to continue rustling up the bran flakes on a long-term basis.

Also, often when a woman is doing a bit of idle Forward Planning, an image of herself . . . alone . . . on a Friday night . . . in a very small flat . . . having a birthday with four or more in it flashes before her. (Adding a cat to this image isn't always comforting.) The woman thinks that a cutie in the kitchen might be an antidote to this image. She'd like to know what Mr Cutie himself thinks. She doesn't want to pressure him, you understand. She just wants to *know* (so she can decide whether she ought to reconsider the cat).

reading his horoscope

AND, TOMORROW, EVERY MAN BORN UNDER THE SIGN OF PISCES WILL PROPOSE TO A WOMAN WITH UNMANAGEABLE HAIR

What are you thinking?

When a woman wants to know something like this she mentally runs through her options. These are her options:

- Relying on a tried-and-tested technique
- Analysing everything he does and has done since they met. (This list would include items not immediately obvious to the uninitiated, e.g. he went quiet, he didn't send his Valentine till after 3 p.m. and he had this sort of 'look' on his face.)
- Analysing everything he says and has said since they met
- Analysing everything his friends say and have said since they met
- Asking him directly. Women who are in the early stages of relationships are very, very nervous about this option unless they live in New York. Men who live in New York are very, very nervous

OK, wait, don't tell me. I know this one.

Often, a woman doesn't want to ask a man something directly, she'd rather Talk Things Over.

talking things over

When a woman wants to get a man more *verbally* involved in a relationship, she relies on three basic methods.

The canary

The woman just chatters on to the man about anything that comes into her head. She goes into plenty of detail. She figures that, eventually, something she says will catch his attention and he will chip in.

The man is *amazed* at the woman's ability to keep talking. He only responds minimally and intermittently. He doesn't remember a word she says. (The woman is *amazed* by this – 'But I *told* you . . .')

The mosquito

The woman punctuates her chatter with specific enquiries. These enquiries are aimed directly at the man with the intention of needling him out of what seems to the woman like a semi-comatose state.

The man, who is very busy watching a rerun of a children's science-fiction programme on the television, ignores the buzzing for as long as he can. Eventually he swats at it: '*WHAT?*'

There is a Mosquito variant in which the woman's probes have to do with the man's feelings for her. This tactic usually fails to get a man's attention, especially if he is still very busy with the children's science-fiction rerun. Eventually, the woman gets fed up with the lack of response to her subtle enquiries and starts to make up the answers for herself. She says things like: 'You *obviously* don't care about me at all'.

The man ignores her for as long as possible. Then he figures that she must have put an awful lot of thought into this since she's always going on about it. He begins to believe her.

By the time a woman figures out this sequence of events, it is usually too late.

The big cat

The woman waits until the man is in a vulnerable position. Then she pounces. Favourite vulnerable positions are traffic jams, supper times and bed.

GETTING THINGS STRAIGHT

number of players: *two*
ONE MALE, *unsuspecting*
ONE FEMALE, *determined*

object
MALE: to avoid this conversation
FEMALE: to find out where she stands

points scored by
MALE: for deflecting direct enquiries without starting a row
FEMALE: for breaking through male defences without starting a row

catchphrases
- *Do you realise that on Tuesday it will be exactly eighteen months since we met?*
- *Going on like this . . .*
- *Thirty years old . . .*

points deducted for
MALE:
- *ending the conversation abruptly*
- *ending the conversation abruptly and switching on the television/picking up a newspaper/leaving the room*
FEMALE:
- *Insisting on continuing the conversation after the male has ended it abruptly*

characteristic moves

FEMALE: rehearses her tactics in advance and then relies on the element of surprise to draw the male into the game: often she waits till she has him in a corner where there are no televisions, newspapers or visible means of escape

MALE: relies initially on evasive tactics and will go to some lengths to avoid actual confrontation: in order to achieve this he may have to cheat, i.e. lie

advanced moves

MALE: allows the female to play the entire game by herself. He makes no moves whatsoever. She supplies his responses. Thus, the male maintains his position while the female gains the impression that progress has been made (this level of skill is usually only attained by experienced players)

I do want to talk about it some more, but it's only six hours until the match starts.

The man develops some expert deflecting tactics involving maps, newspapers and very deep sleep (the feigning thereof).

It doesn't matter what method a woman uses, at some point in her relationship she will hear herself say:

'You haven't heard a word I've said, have you?'

Quite often it's a short, slippery slope from here to:

'If you won't tell me what's wrong, how can I help?'
and:

'But we talked about this and you **agreed** . . .'

Women sometimes forget that in a conversation more than one person talks. Women don't need to be reminded of the arguments they've had with men because they assumed that saying 'Uh-huh' on a sporadic basis *was* talking.

Actually, a man isn't always completely unresponsive. A man can tell the difference between the times when a woman is imparting some specific information (with a beginning, a middle and an end) and the times when she is just, well, talking . . . Women don't always make this distinction. So usually if a woman is telling a man that she has a problem (so that he will understand), he listens. He does this for about two thirds of the time that it takes for the woman to do the telling. Then he interrupts her and offers a solution. This solution is encapsulated in two briskly delivered sentences.

The woman is convinced that he will *never* understand.

The man does not know that the only response required in circumstances like these is: 'Choco-mocha chip or double pecan fudge?'

ASK AUNT LOLA
ADVICE FOR THE
LOVELORN

Dear Aunt Lola

My boyfriend pays no attention to me when I'm talking. What can I do?

Sugar, these are the rules for formal public speaking:

1) Tell 'em what you're gonna tell 'em
2) Tell 'em
3) Tell 'em what you've told 'em

Do this in under five minutes.

Aunt Lola suggests applying these guidelines in all verbal exchanges with men.

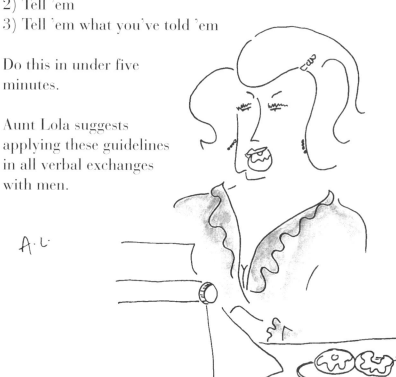

THROWING A WOBBLY

number of players: *any number from two . . .*
ONE MALE
ONE FEMALE, who was really looking forward to this evening
Most of the diners in a crowded restaurant

object
MALE: to make it stop
*FEMALE: not always clear but it seems to matter an awful lot at the
time*

points scored by
MALE: for remaining seated and silent throughout the proceedings
*FEMALE: for managing to convince herself, the male, and the other
restaurant diners that anybody would behave this way under
these circumstances (as yet unclear to the other diners, who
begin to make side bets)*

catchphrases
■ *sentences containing the word 'selfish'*
■ *sentences containing expletives*
■ *sentences containing the word 'selfish' and an expletive*

points deducted for
MALE:
■ *saying 'Have you calmed down now?'*
FEMALE:
■ *wimping out halfway through a full-blown showdown and
starting to snivel instead*

characteristic moves

FEMALE: wakes up the next morning, takes stock and rethinks her position. She cannot remember quite how she got there. She makes some let's-be-friends-ish moves towards the male

MALE: backs off. He looks at the female as if she were an alien from another planet, and makes it clear that it is likely to be quite some time before he is convinced otherwise

advanced moves

MALE: deliberately chooses a public place, such as a crowded restaurant, and then makes the opening move himself. He is betting that the female will not make a major countermove due to the proximity of the other diners. When this gambit fails, the results are spectacular

There are women who choose to test a man's devotion via very indirect means. These means tend towards the devious.

testing a man's devotion via devious means

If you really loved me

I married you, didn't I?

The woman chooses something to which the man is very obviously attached (activity or object), then she tries to get him to give it up, or to her. She starts out quite subtly:

- 'I don't see why you have to go *every* Saturday'
- 'It's *just* a car'

But the pace soon hots up:

That was a week ago.

- 'If you *really* loved me . . .'

The man usually has to have a little think at this stage.

NB: Sometimes a woman is not playing 'If you really loved me' at all. It's just that she truly cannot imagine ever getting so caught up in the pursuit of the perfect putt that she would forget her boyfriend's birthday.

You're not the only fish in the sea, you know

The woman:
- Flirts madly and openly with some other chap
- Alludes to a mysterious admirer (sometimes this admirer actually exists; he has halitosis)
- Refers to someone on the telly, or the number nineteen bus, as 'dishy'

The man says: 'I can't believe you spent all night gassing to that idiot with halitosis.' Secretly, he has a little think.

Moving right along

I'm getting married next spring and you are the lucky man.

The woman announces some sort of 'twosome' plan in public. This announcement implies that the man and woman have a relationship which is established, solid and ongoing. It can be anything with the word 'we' in it but sometimes it has a word like 'engaged' in it too.

A man who doesn't think about this at the time usually finds himself pondering at length once the honeymoon is over.

When a woman considers that a relationship is not on an altogether firm footing (this can happen after fourteen years and four kids), she usually feels it would be wise to be vigilant with regard to Other Women.

leaving something at his house that another woman will spot immediately

And then he left his job, collected his life savings, dumped his wife and kids and ran off with a barmaid called Angie.

If a man says anything like 'It just happened' a woman is absolutely furious with him. A woman thinks that a man is a grown-up human being with a will of his own. She doesn't see why he couldn't have thought about not-meaning-to-hurt-her before he went ahead and did whatever it was. Whatever it was generally has something to do with another woman.

The thing is, despite the grown-up-human-being-with-a-will-of-his-own claim, most women have seen enough evidence to the contrary to be wary. A woman doesn't have to look very far to find a fellow who risked his life/wife/kids/career for the sake of a bit of titty that 'didn't mean anything'. So women tend to keep a reasonably close eye on any bits of titty that are knocking about within just-happening distance of their men.

They'll do that, you know.

protecting him from predators

OOH LOOK, THERE'S SUE AND JAMES

A man often assumes that a woman is Irrationally Jealous of every other woman in his life. This is nonsense. The woman is only irrationally jealous of women with whom the man already has a history.

Whoa ... what made her blow up like that?

Re women with whom men already have a history: women sympathise with Daphne Du Maurier's heroine in *Rebecca* because, poor cookie, she's married to a man who's carrying a torch for his ex. Women breathe a sigh of relief when they discover that the fellow actually *loathed* said ex, to the point of doing her in.

An old flame.

Murderer v. Man Who Is Still In Love With His Ex. No contest.

The problems with regard to women with whom men already have a history are exacerbated if a woman meets a man at a stage in his life when another woman is not history at all. A man isn't always terribly forthcoming about the exact details of this situation. Mostly, he prefers to let a woman have the fun of figuring it out for herself.

In cases like these, the man is usually keen to make sure that the relationship with woman number two is on a very firm footing indeed before he whips his slippers out from under woman number one. While he is doing this, woman number one gets progressively more *suspicious* and woman number two comes up with a New Plan every four and a half minutes.

Woman number two treats this period like a sort of audition.

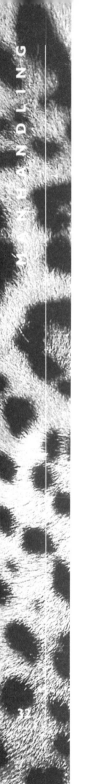

Dear Aunt Lola

My no-good husband has run off and left me penniless.

Darlin', did you confuse marriage with life assurance?

auditioning

The man implies that woman number one is a bit of a nagging old cow. 'She's so *suspicious*,' he confides to woman number two.

Woman number two does her absolute best at not acting suspicious.

'She gives me such a hard time,' complains the man.

Woman number two gives her no-hard-time-at-all performance.

The man throws in a few miscellaneous complaints with regard to things like smoking and sports.

Take it from me, mate. Never hang around long enough to find out their last names.

The world is remarkably short of women who say 'You must be a nightmare to live with' at this stage.

The man is eventually convinced that woman number two is going to be pretty easy to live with. He leaves woman number one four and a half minutes later.

That's B-O-B-B-I-T.

Woman number two *is* pretty easy to live with until the day (about four days later) when the man tells her what a decent soul he thinks woman number one is.

Re decent souls: a man is usually of the opinion that a woman he's just ditched for another woman is, in fact, a pretty decent soul (that's why he didn't want to hurt her). Sometimes a woman does something which leaves a fairly solid dent in his opinion. This sort of something:

- Something to do with scissors and suits
- Something to do with extremely smelly cheese and the boot of a car

- Something to do with grass seed and carpet
- Something to do with the speaking clock in another country and a telephone

But sometimes she doesn't. Sometimes she just behaves like a pretty decent soul, which exacerbates the irrational jealousy problem of the new woman like mad.

harbouring no resentment towards his past loves

The other women in the man's life that a woman dislikes intensely are women she distrusts. Often this distrust is very rational indeed.

A woman distrusts slags, slappers, tramps, tarts, trollops and bimbos.

She can spot one of these by her lack of clothing and abundance of make-up. A man can spot one too.

A woman deals with a slag, slapper, tramp, tart, trollop or bimbo threat by pointing out what a slag, slapper, tramp, tart, trollop or bimbo the woman is the moment the man spots her. She goes on to point this out at every opportunity.

When a woman is not physically with a man, she discourages him from frequenting places which are frequented by slags, slappers, tramps, tarts, trollops and bimbos. She does this by asking the man subtle questions like:

'Will any of the other wives or girlfriends be there?'

and:

'Where were you last night?'

monitoring his movements

WHERE HAVE
YOU BEEN

Once a woman is in a reasonably established relationship with a man, she usually lets up a bit with regard to slag, slapper, tramp, tart, trollop and bimbo alert. This is because:

I'm not looking
for a husband.

Decided to try a
bachelor for a
change, have you?

1 The man has agreed with her whenever she has pointed out what a slag, slapper, tramp, tart, trollop or bimbo some woman is
2 She knows that if it really came to the crunch (heaven forbid) she could fight a slag, slapper, tramp, tart, trollop or bimbo and win

A woman is not so confident with regard to a Queen B. All women know a Queen B when they see one. Mostly, men haven't got the first clue.

A Queen B has no woman code; she goes after any man she wants. She stings rivals to death. A Queen B is a cool customer. Often she looks awfully inviting to a man with a stressed-out wife and three kids.

A woman has to be clever if a Queen B is keen on her man.

Sometimes she makes a mistake.

Examples of mistakes a woman makes

■ Calling the Queen B a slag, slapper, tramp, tart, trollop or bimbo. The man, on account of no lack-of-clothes or abundance-of-make-up clues, considers this unfair, unpleasant and witchy

■ Pointing out to the man that the Queen B is *after* him and *obviously* fancies him like mad. Very few men, especially ones with stressed-out wives and/or three kids, can resist being fancied like mad

Sometimes she just relies on the following tried-and-tested techniques:

■ Avoiding all social contact with known Queen Bs: 'I will not have that woman in my house'

■ Being extra sweet to her man if she suspects he's in the beeline

■ Making it *clear* to the B, and the man, and everyone else in the vicinity, that they are a couple ('with kids' is useful here)

■ Holding out and hoping

All women who have lost a man to another woman consider that this woman is a slag, slapper, tramp, tart, trollop, bimbo or complete old witch of a Queen B.

This is because women are not at all keen on the notion that their man had been meaning to leave them for ages but didn't get around to it until he fell in love with a perfectly nice woman from the stationery suppliers.

Eventually, a woman comes to trust that a man is reasonably immune to the slag, slapper, tramp, tart, trollop, bimbo, Queen B and scheming ex threat. As a general rule she is not just depending on his word.

A woman has a whole host of techniques for keeping track of a man. For example, in the early days, when a woman is still not getting as many clues from a man as she'd like, she might take to calling him in the morning. (After fourteen years and four kids she finds this particular technique handy for business trips and sports away days.)

dawn calling

Of course I trust him. I was just checking up on him.

A woman knows that a man is unlikely to try the popped-out-for-cigarettes line at 7.41 a.m. So she uses this classic casual scrutiny tactic if she is suspicious or if *he* hasn't called *her*. Often this amounts to the same thing.

When the woman dials the man's digits at 7.41 a.m. she is looking for two things:

1 Him:
   Beeep . . . 'Oh, hi . . . it's me. It's about, I don't know (7.41 precisely, you ratbag) eightish . . .'

2 The Telltale-Telephone-Tone-Tip-Off:.

When a woman has called a man at a time when it is inconvenient (7.41 a.m.) and he has picked up the phone (because he is in a hotel room in Australia and hasn't really thought things through), he doesn't say 'Hello, love' in his normal sweet, sleepy, happy-to-hear-from-you voice. He says:

'Hi ... how are you?'

in his bumping-into-an-old-school-friend, what-a-surprise voice. Or he says:

'I'll call you back'

in his someone-from-the-desk-making-an-inane-enquiry-about-luggage voice.

Either way, a woman is on to him.

If the man does say 'Hello, love' in his normal sweet, sleepy, happy-to-hear-from-you voice, the woman feels all her suspiciousness ebb away. She feels much better. She gives him a load of earache about not calling her.

A woman who is feeling reassured gives up on scrutiny for a while. This would last for ages if nothing ever happened to put her on Red Alert.

Sometimes a woman is on constant Red Alert. This is because she's insecure, or very, very suspicious indeed. A man knows when he's dealing with a woman in this state because if he smiles at his third cousin once removed at a Christmas party, she says something like:

'You're sleeping with her, aren't you?'

TELLING HIM OFF

number of players: *two*
ONE MALE, *unsure what the big deal is*
ONE FEMALE, *with every reason to be cross*

object
MALE: *to get back into the good books with as little effort as possible*
FEMALE: *to impress upon the male that this type of behaviour is unacceptable and won't be tolerated in the future*

points scored by
MALE: *for apologising and making a sincere attempt not to repeat said unacceptable behaviour for a period of longer than two weeks in duration*
FEMALE: *for stating her case in under thirteen minutes*

catchphrases
- That is not the point
- I've got better things to do
- A bit more consideration . . .

points deducted for
MALE:
- *saying 'give it a rest, won't you'*
FEMALE:
- *not giving it a rest*

characteristic moves
FEMALE: *maintains her position steadfastly*
MALE: *favours ducking and diving over backtracking*

A man is not a fool. A man has a whole host of techniques for putting a woman who is on Red Alert off the scent:

'What? That old slaggy slapper, tramp, tart, trollop of a bimbo ... give me a break.'

Plus, a man suspects that all women are pretty nosy. So if he has something he'd like to keep secret, he puts it away carefully in his wardrobe, desk or briefcase.

A woman on Red Alert laughs in the face of such naivety.

keeping him under surveillance

Things a woman has done because she is on Red Alert

- Opened a man's briefcase
- Rifled through the contents of a man's briefcase
- Spent a long time trying to remember what the contents of the man's briefcase looked like before she rifled through them
- Called last-number redial
- Called last-number redial and hung up when a woman answered

He thinks I spy on him.

- Read a telephone bill
- Called a number on the telephone bill
- Read a diary
- Tried to figure out what 'M 3.15' means
- Looked in a man's bedside drawer
- Counted condoms
  - Looked through a man's desk
  - Had something that felt very like a heart attack because the phone rang when she was looking through a man's desk

Did he say something to you about it?

  - Followed a man
  - Had a man followed
- Phoned a hotel where a man was staying and waited a very, very long time while someone tried to find him
- Continued to phone the hotel where a man was staying on a half-hourly basis ('I'll hold')
- Showed up at a hotel where a man was staying
- Phoned a fishing lodge (ditto)
- Held an envelope up to the light
- Spent a very long time trying to read the postmark on an envelope

No, it was in his diary.

- Opened an envelope
- Had a panic and chucked the contents of the envelope in the bin

- Interrogated a man's colleagues and friends
- Made an extremely casual, you-don't-say sort of comment in order to draw a bit more information out of a man's colleagues or friends
- Looked through a man's pockets
- Read a credit card bill
- Read cheque stubs
- Listened to an answering-machine tape
- Actually removed an answering-machine tape and taken it home to listen to it
- Searched a car's glove compartment
- Had a more than casual shufti through a man's bathroom cabinet
- Measured how much moisturiser is left in the bottle she keeps in a man's bathroom cabinet
- Removed a hair from a hairbrush and compared it to her own
- Checked a man's clothes for traces of lipstick
- Sniffed a man's clothes (for traces of other things)
- Checked sheets (ditto)
- Checked a man's body (ditto)
- Looked through a waste-paper basket
- Uncrumpled a piece of message paper which is in the waste-paper basket and tried to figure out what 'M 555 4493' means
- Called 555 4493
- Hung up when a man answered
- Had a bit of a panic because the man who answered might call last-number redial
- Picked up the kitchen telephone extension
- Had what felt very like a heart attack when she heard the conversation the man was having with the wife of one of their friends

A woman does these things for two reasons:

> I want to know who's responsible for his happiness.

1 To prove to herself that a man isn't at it
2 To have the upper hand if he is

On the day that a woman catches a man at it, her heart is broken.

But, for the first time in a fair old while, she figures she has the upper hand. She is keen to exploit this situation for as long as possible. She lets the man get himself a wee bit further down into the mire before she confronts him.

The woman comes out of the kitchen and says 'Who was that?' in an extremely casual sort of way, and the man tells her it was his squash partner. Then the woman says 'Uh huh' in a you-don't-say sort of way. She manages to keep this cool, collected upper-hand approach going for about another twenty-four seconds.

'I HEARD you!'

(Often it's a short, slippery slope from here to a sentence with the word slag, slapper, tramp, tart, trollop or bimbo in it.)

A woman doesn't delve through drawers if she just doesn't want to know. Usually this means that she already knows (fourteen years and four kids could be a feature here). This woman gets on with her life and ignores the obvious.

ASK AUNT LOLA
ADVICE FOR THE
SNAPPY LOVELORN

Dear Aunt Lola

I found out my boyfriend has been having an affair with a woman at his office for two years. When I confronted him about it he got really upset. He swears it's all over now. He says it's me he wants. I'm so confused, I don't know what to do.

Oh yes you
doooo . . .

A·L

ignoring the obvious

The obvious:

- Large sums of money   appearing/disappearing
- Women's underwear   appearing/disappearing
- A man   appearing/disappearing (for longer than it takes to pop out for cigarettes)

A woman who just doesn't want to know about any of the above often finds that it isn't long before somebody tells her. This somebody is never a man.

giving him the benefit of the doubt

THERE YOU ARE, LOVE
I WAS JUST COMING TO
LOOK FOR YOU

Often the slag, slapper, tramp, tart, trollop, bimbo, scheming ex or perfectly nice woman from the stationery suppliers who has fallen for a man who is otherwise engaged finds herself doing a very long audition. In between best-behaviour performances she usually follows these tried-and-tested techniques for:

wooing a married man

- Believing everything he says for the first twenty-five minutes
- Believing nothing he says for the rest of the relationship
- Really trying to believe some of the things he says for the very brief periods in between

We're married in name only.

Lots of these have to do with 'soon'.

That would be the name on the company share certificates, pension scheme, insurance documents, car registration, mortgage and children's birth certificates, I guess.

Sometimes a woman decides that soon isn't soon enough. She gets desperate (often with the help of her friends and a bottle of white wine). She decides to try to speed things up a bit. She Phones His Home Number.

When a woman Phones His Home Number, one of these things happens:

1 She loses her nerve (the woman at the other end goes on to Red Alert)
2 She doesn't (the woman at the other end says, *'You've been sleeping with her, haven't you?'* very soon afterwards)

The mere thought of this possibility is enough to bring the average man out in hives.

Quite often at some point during the Wooing a Married Man scenario, woman number two says, *'You've been sleeping with her, haven't you?'* She is referring to woman number one. In these circumstances, a man always issues an emphatic denial. This is the thing woman number two tries her absolute hardest to believe.

A Queen B is usually much too cool for these sorts of games. A Queen B plays Throwing Down the Gauntlet.

throwing down the gauntlet

Won't your girlfriend miss you?

A woman knows that a man has a hard time resisting a challenge. Some women are not above using this characteristic to their advantage.

'I'll bet you're the kind of man who'd never leave his wife.'

There is a Throwing Down the Gauntlet variation which has nothing to do with Wooing a Married Man. It's this:

'Well, I guess I'll just have to ask my father/brother/best friend's husband/that hunk I know from the gym . . .'

It doesn't matter what kind of woman a man is playing away with, he almost always claims to be the innocent party when things start hitting the fan, the walls and him.

Unfortunately, she's a pretty good shot.

'It just happened.'

Sometimes a man gets lucky and woman number one swallows this line. It almost chokes her. This woman plays:

standing by your man

Darling, I want to come clean about my infidelities.

It is mostly women who are married to men in the public eye who do Standing By Your Man. This involves grinning, in a grimacy kind of way, and letting the press and public see that you are a twenty-year-older but otherwise exact replica of another woman (she is not called this behind closed doors) who the man has been Lying By.

Every now and then the woman who the man in the public eye has been Lying By plays dirty. (Women can never believe that a man didn't see this coming: 'You only need to look at her to see she's a . . .') The scheming little slag, slapper, tramp, trollop, right tart of a bimbo decides it's worth:

We went through all this last night.

Since then.

spilling the beans for bucks

The mere thought of this possibility is enough to bring the average man in the public eye out in bubonic plague.

Ordinary folks are much more likely to stick with:

keeping up appearances

This also involves grinning in a grimacy kind of way, and letting your friends see that you have not had a right barney in the car on the way over. The woman tends to do about twice as much grimacy grinning as the man, which is a dead giveaway to all her friends that the couple have had a right barney in the car on the way over.

Luckily for everyone's sanity, there are lots of times in relationships when nobody is playing away and hardly anyone is suspicious at all.

In circumstances like these, a man often finds himself coming in for a good bit of Absolute Adoration.

absolute adoration

When a woman is a girl, she practises Absolute Adoration techniques on posters of pop stars, the bathroom mirror and the back of her hand.

You say the sweetest things.

Sometimes a horse gets very lucky.

You say the sweetest things.

When a woman is all grown up she gets to put her practice to good use on a man. The man loves the Absolute Adoration. As long as he's feeling Absolutely Adored he is pretty much putty in the

You say the sweetest things.

woman's hands. The woman thinks that if he keeps being this sweet and putty-like it will be very easy indeed to go on Absolutely Adoring him for ever.

Yeah, yeah.

49

Then this happens:

The man decides that all this Absolute Adoration is lovely but he'd quite like to have some of it from afar (like a pop star) so that he can get on with other things. ('I'm watching this.')

And this happens:

The man decides that he can take the Absolute Adoration but not the Constant Romantic Gestures. A woman doesn't always make the distinction.

entertaining his friends

DINNER IS SERVED, GENTLEMEN

Examples of Constant Romantic Gestures

- Hundreds of honey-bunny phone calls
- Little cards and pressies
- More little cards and pressies
- Masses and masses of kisses and 'missed you's

Constant Romantic Gestures make men feel squirmy because:

1 They know they are expected to respond. (Sometimes they're busy. Sometimes they're lazy. Sometimes they're hazy as to what their response is meant to be.)
2 They think these things have their place. (This place is not usually the lobby of their office building or the number nineteen bus.)

A woman doesn't always make the distinction.

Often when a woman has given a man a ton of Absolute Adoration only to have him say 'Not here, OK?' she decides that she will only dole it out on a really and truly deserved basis thereafter.

Some women confuse Absolute Adoration with Absolute Attachment.

doing things 'as a couple'

Some women confuse Absolute Adoration with:

agreeing with absolutely everything he says

The woman who opts for Agreeing With Absolutely
Everything He Says often favours Trying To Be Absolutely
Everything He Wants In A Woman, too. The man who hangs
around after the onset of this kind of behaviour usually wants
something flat that you keep by a door.

Most women aren't nearly so daft.

Things a sane woman has done because she is in love

- Shaved her legs on a very regular basis
- Read the Valentine's breakfast
  recipes in a women's magazine
- Actually made the heart-shaped
  smoked salmon thingies in the recipe
- Bought herself an item of clothing that she would have
  to be in love to wear
    - Gone to work in an item of clothing which
      she first put on over twelve hours ago
    - Worn stockings with a cavalier disregard for
      Visible Suspender Line
- Spent quite a bit of money on potions and lotions for
  looking gorgeous
- Spent quite a bit of time ensuring she looks as gorgeous
  as possible
- Rearranged herself on a chair or a bed so as to look
  more gorgeous
- Brushed her teeth at 5 a.m.
- Put a slushy Post-It note on a bathroom mirror

Is that you, honey-bun?

Yes, who's this?

■ Developed a sudden interest in jazz
■ Cried over something extremely silly
■ Laughed over something extremely silly
■ Rushed to the letter box with an eagerness bordering on the absurd
■ Agreed to watch a film in which more than twenty-seven people come to a grisly end
■ Lost weight
■ Gained weight
■ Bought a card with very few sensible words on it
■ Had a lot more telephone conversations than normal
■ Had a telephone conversation with very few sensible words in it
■ Kissed a telephone . . . a photograph . . . an envelope . . .
■ Not slept
■ Slept very, very late
■ Eaten pasta in bed (with a cavalier disregard for the bedding)
■ Fed someone who was over the age of five from her own fork
■ Tried to stop herself from thinking that a man might have had an accident because he is late
■ Tried to stop herself from thinking about any of the other reasons he might be late which pop, unbidden, into her mind
■ Moved to Hong Kong

Are you all right, dear?

No, I'm in love.

A sane modern woman who realises that men sometimes react badly to *constant* Constant Romantic Gestures is careful not to overdo the above. She waits until the man does some of them for her. Eventually, the man does one of them for her. Then the woman thinks it will be OK to do three of them for him in return (she waits twenty-five minutes before she does this). In between she Gives Him Some Space.

53

LEAVING THEM TO IT

number of players: three
TWO MALES, *slightly inebriated*
ONE FEMALE, *tired*

object
MALES: *to get more inebriated*
FEMALE: *to get some sleep*

points scored by
MALES: *for solving all the ills of the world during the hours
    between 1 and 4 a.m.*
FEMALE: *for being mature and sophisticated enough to encourage
    her male to have some fun without her . . . while
    simultaneously implying that this kind of fun is immature and
    unsophisticated*

catchphrases
- Night, night, then, you two
- Don't forget to switch off the lights, love
- Remember you've got to get up in the morning

Points deducted for
MALES:
- *forgetting to switch off the lights*
- *not getting up in the morning*
- *loud crashing noises during the hours between 1 and 4 a.m.*

FEMALE:

- *giving people a hard time about something that nobody gives a monkey's about, like lights, for heaven's sake*
- *using violent means to get people up*
- *coming down to investigate a particularly loud crashing noise at 3 a.m. wearing an old dressing gown and a frown*

characteristic moves

FEMALE: upon delivering the night-night-then-you-two line gives her male a bit of a kiss and a look. This kiss and look implies either (a) Wake me when you come up and don't be too long, I'll be waiting, handsome; or (b) I am absolutely shattered, on no account wake me when you come up

MALE: misreads these signals and thus forfeits his right to play again in the foreseeable future

A man sometimes feels that *he* is being kept in the dark with regard to the future of a relationship. (Sometimes this future only extends till breakfast tomorrow, but still . . .) In these circumstances a man might accuse a woman of Leading Him On.

leading him on

There are women who manipulate men. Usually they manipulate their children, their friends and restaurant maître d's as well. Women dislike them even more than men do. Apart from manipulators, there are two other types of women that men accuse of Leading Them On (this is not the expression they use when they are talking to other men). They are wrong on both counts.

The teenage temptress

Little girls sometimes get big girls' eyes and thighs and breast sizes way before the inside of them is ready to deal with the impact these developments can have on a man.

Adult men sometimes get themselves all tanked up and mistake made up with grown up.

The perfectly nice woman who is really, really trying her best to fancy a nice guy

But she can't. This woman reminds herself of all the rogues, ratbags, bad boys, married men and double-dealing two-timers she's fallen for in the past. She really, really tries even harder. (Her friends urge her on in this endeavour by reminding her of all the rogues, ratbags, bad boys, married men and double-dealing two-timers she's fallen for in the

OK, listen, number three . . . would you consider having a relationship with any of the following: A a killer on Death Row; B a werewolf; C a man with grey shoes who rolls his umbrella up neatly and puts it in a plastic bag?

past: '*And* that other one . . . you *do* remember, the one with the wife in Mauritius.')

And while she is really, really trying, she keeps saying yes to the nice guy when he calls.

She doesn't put a great deal of effort into ensuring that he *keeps* calling. A woman really, really wishes that she could be this relaxed when she has fallen for some rogue, ratbag, bad boy, married man, double-dealing two-timer or even just some fellow with a *very* cute smile (who is probably one of the above). But she *can't.*

Can A dance?

What kind of car does B drive?

Sometimes a woman isn't Leading A Man On. She's just flirting with a Spanish waiter which everyone knows doesn't count. Or it could be that she likes a man a lot but she's:

keeping him in a holding pattern

It's like this:

There are plenty of men in the world who fall in love.

There are plenty of men in the world who fall in love fast.

Anyone who doubts this need only note the amount of time it takes for a bloke with a broken leg to propose to a pretty nurse.

The thing is that the pretty nurse has rather a nice life and nice friends and a nice flat. Still, she is awfully keen on the chap, so she thinks hard about for ever and having a lot fewer nice Friday nights in on her own. Then, one day, she catches the number nineteen bus to work and spends a harrowing twenty-seven minutes observing the antics of a mother of toddlers. An image of herself in a very small flat with two under two flashes before her.

When a woman has a nice flat, a nice life and some doubts about breastfeeding, she doesn't discourage Mr Cutie. She doesn't encourage him either. She's quite happy with the way things are.

The man hovers happily for quite a while. He might drop the odd hint with regard to the future of the relationship, and possibly offspring, but he doesn't push it.

Then, one day, the woman is feeling a bit angry, a bit unhappy, a bit flabby or a bit drab, and she has a go at him about the fact that he has never even *suggested* they put the relationship on a firm footing.

> *We're all looking for the perfect man, love, but you may as well get married in the meantime.*

A man might have accused a woman of Leading Him On because she touched him . . . on the number nineteen bus in the rush hour. This is the kind of man who cannot handle being given the brush-off.

When women are young they ditch bores, and Spanish waiters who've got the wrong idea, by climbing out of loo windows and legging it across car parks. The presence of a friend enhances an adventure like this enormously. But as women get older, they tend not to risk their dignity, or their tights, quite so readily. They do this instead:

giving him the brush-off

So, how come a gorgeous girl like you isn't married?

- Glaring in a how-dare-you kind of way (often interpreted by men as 'I am a lesbian')
- Sneering in an in-your-dreams kind of way (often interpreted by men as 'Please call me darling')
- Giggling ('Gagging for it')
- Issuing a clear verbal command containing an expletive ('Please call me a lesbian who is gagging for it and waggle your crotch at me')

Just lucky, I guess.

In the end a woman tends to give up on the above and rely on these tried-and-tested techniques:

- Staring at the ground
- Muttering something about a boyfriend in Australia (not all men are completely convinced by the boyfriend in Australia line. Not all women think of it in time. That's why most women have been out with a slightly overweight, shy accountant with clammy hands)

In films, women are always dealing with men who get nasty like this:

- Throwing drinks in their faces
- Throwing spaghetti in their laps
- Whacking them one, square on the chops, in a public place

A lot of women can think of an occasion when all three might have been appropriate. They wish they'd given them a whirl, but usually they were trying too hard not to cry at the time.

Why did the woman cross the road?

The thing is that in real life, although all women feel very, very angry at a man at some point, there are a lot more points when they're just sort of irritated. Unfortunately for men, this reaction is not reserved for people perched perilously on scaffolding who think they are God's gift to any woman wearing boots.

Hello, darling, give us a smile …

Oh, come on, sweetheart, cheer up, it might never 'appen …

'Ere, tell you what, I've got something that'll put a grin on your face ..

the if-you-weren't-listening-the-first-time response

OH, NEVER MIND WHAT I SAID

Sometimes a woman gets irritated about having to say things more than once. Sometimes a woman gets irritated because of the way a man holds his knife. Sometimes a woman gets irritated because the man who *keeps* calling is a clammy-handed accountant instead of some rogue, ratbag, bad boy, married man or double-dealing two-timer with a *very* cute smile. Add a lousy haircut to any of this and what you have is an extremely Off Day.

A perfectly nice man is often on the end of one.

A man knows when a woman is having an Off Day because he comes in for a bit of Aural Abuse.

aural abuse

What's my problem? Well, let's see. I can't stand the way you use a fork and I can't shoot you.

Most women have a capacity for verbal warfare that most men can't match. Generally they keep this capacity under their hats. But sometimes the whole flabby, drab, bad-haircut, terrible-table-manners thing just gets on top of a woman. She can't help it. She lets fly.

'Do you have to do that?'

When a man first feels the sting of a nasty remark he doesn't immediately fling back a little dart of his own. Usually he just goes quiet and licks his wound.

The woman looks at him, an unsuspecting man, a soft target. She knows that she has behaved badly. She feels . . . powerful. A woman who doesn't have this feeling too often might get addicted to it. She is likely to become a very sharp-tongued creature indeed. Mostly, though, a woman keeps the

LULLING HIM INTO A FALSE SENSE OF SECURITY

number of players: *two*
ONE MALE, slightly nervous
ONE FEMALE, slightly grumpy

object
*MALE: to find out whether he will be in big trouble if he
does/doesn't do something*
*FEMALE: to give the impression that she couldn't care less what he
does, and why would he be 'in trouble' anyway, he is not a child*

points scored by
MALE: for getting out of the door before she changes her mind
*FEMALE: for saying one thing whilst simultaneously implying the
exact opposite*

catchphrases
- *Go ahead*
- *When have I ever minded ...*
- *I've said, it's fine*

points deducted for

MALE:

■ *paying attention to any of the above*

■ *reminding people that they said any of the above*

FEMALE:

■ *denying ever saying any of the above*

characteristic moves

FEMALE: having delivered her go-ahead-when-have-I-ever-minded-I've-said-it's-fine line does not give the male any sort of kiss at all when he is racing out the door

MALE: attempts to rectify this situation but has a sneaking suspicion that the complete lack of response to his attempt is a harbinger of doom. He gambles everything on being wrong. This is a high-stakes move

sharpest edge of her tongue under control. This is more of a struggle than any man knows.

In general, men so loathe the idea of getting a load of earache about anything that the mere threat of this possibility is enough to encourage them to keep certain behaviour in check.

I'll never meet a man who can sink to my level.

Because women are thwarted so often with regard to the whacking-them-one-square-on-the-chops-in-a-public-place scenario, and because women spend so much of their time biting their tongues, they tend to develop a truckload of other ways of expressing their irritation with men.

Things a woman has done because she is irritated with a man

- Flirted with one of his friends
- Slept on the very, very edge of the bed
- Sighed loudly when he said something
- Worn jogging trousers
- Worn jogging trousers and not removed any of the hair from her body for quite some time
- Spat in his water glass
- Driven hell out of his car
- Parked his car under a tree with a lot of birds in it
- Mocked and scoffed at his hobby
- Said something unkind about something from the animal kingdom to which he is ridiculously attached
- Made plans that don't include him
- Made it obvious to him that she has plans that don't include him
- Made a big show getting all dolled up in something very different from jogging trousers before going out on the plan that doesn't include him

- Done some very noisy tidying up
- Put a whole lot of his things in
  a big pile during the noisy
  tidying up
- Given him a more-vigorous-than-
  necessary wallop because he was snoring

*I could eat
a horse.*

*Good,
that's what you're
having.*

There are lots of urban legends about cooking
and catfood.

Sometimes a woman is tempted.

If you added a really good haircut and some pretty foxy boots
to the above, you could be dealing with a woman who is:

having an affair

A woman who is Having An Affair does a lot of the same things
as a man who is Having An Affair, except that she is more likely
to say '*You* obviously didn't care at all' than 'It just happened'.

Men should note, though, that great haircut, new boots and
irritation don't necessarily add up to an affair. Sometimes a
woman has just seen some movie with Uma Thurman in it,
decided, I'm going to get a haircut and boots just like Uma's,
and then been disappointed with the level of change this plan
has wrought in her life.

Something else that a woman *might* do if she was Having
An Affair (but mostly women do a lot less in real life than
they do in the movies) is go to a man's office wearing a fur
coat and garters. This is because:

- A lot of women draw the line at fur
- A lot of men would say 'not here, OK'

Actually, most women are not averse to fitting in with a fellow's fantasies. In fact, plenty of women wish that a fellow had a few more. Women who are thinking this way sometimes try to give a man the hint by strutting about the house wearing things that aren't altogether suitable for doing dishes in, or making suggestions which he is a bit surprised by when they are choosing a video.

However, in the first flush of romance a woman isn't always confident enough to try this kind of thing, so often she just fits in with a fellow physically, full stop. Sometimes this leads to misunderstandings later as to just how much nipple-nibbling a woman can take.

adapting to his technique

The nipple-nibbling misunderstanding is often exacerbated by the faking fib. This is not the only fib that women have in their repertoire.

fibbing

Women tell Sex and Lies fibs just like men. There's:

Did she tell you how many lovers she'd had?

- Four before you
- You were fabulous
- From a loo seat

Partly.

(Mind you, as everybody knows, the biggest fib a woman ever told a man is: Only forty-nine ninety-nine.)

In happy relationships, fibbing diminishes after a bit. Couples like this usually do a reasonable amount of kissing and whispering and hugging and tugging at each other's hands. They do it in public as a kind of 'twosome' announcement. They do it at home too.

The man and woman are happy with this arrangement unless one of them is busy. When a woman is busy, she wiggles her shoulders and says something jokey with the word 'off' in it, the man gives some bit of her a couple more playful squeezes, just because he can, and then goes back to his paper.

Things are not always so simple when a man is busy. A man being busy can bring out the worst in a woman.

piquing his interest

A dog will chew up a cushion just to get attention. When the dog-owner comes home and discovers the chewed-up cushion, she gives the dog a hard time: '*BAD* dog'.

The dog figures that even though this isn't exactly tummy-tickling, it's attention and it will do.

67

When a woman feels she is being taken for granted – i.e. ignored – and also she's *bored*, she is not beyond doing something that will irritate a man intensely just to shift his focus from whatever he is busy with, to her. Often a woman pretends that what she's after is a bit of tummy-tickling. She makes some sort of teasing and only mildly irritating gesture to make this clear (tongue and ear would be a likely combo here). If this is unsuccessful, she ups the ante. A man who is really busy starts to get a wee bit annoyed at this stage. The woman ups the ante again. A barney ensues. It's not tummy-tickling but it will do.

Everybody has heard at least one funny Piquing His Interest story in which a woman comes into the house and is rather shocked to see her husband in the sitting room. This is on account of what she's just done to the man whose legs and lower regions are sticking out from under the car:

> *'No, I couldn't do anything with it,*
> *so I asked Joe to take a look.'*

There are times when a woman becomes increasingly irritated with a man who is increasingly busy. Things have got out of hand.

In circumstances like these, a woman often wakes up one day and feels appalled at what a sharp-tongued creature she has become. She thinks that the relationship might be on its last legs. An image of herself . . . alone . . . on a Friday night . . . in a very small flat . . . having a birthday with four or more in it flashes before her.

The woman decides that having one last go at getting the relationship on to a firm footing might provide an antidote to this image.

ASK AUNT LOLA
ADVICE FOR THE
LOVELORN

Dear Aunt Lola

My boyfriend says he's leaving me. What should I do?

Before he goes, teach him not to treat any part of a woman's body like a radio control dial. This is your gift to sisterhood. Good karma, honey.

A.L

Do you think we'll ever get married?

It should be noted that modern women do not necessarily think that a firm footing has to involve a load of lacy clothes, raisiny cake and drunken uncles. Plenty of modern women would be just as happy with a nice little shift dress and a taxi to the town hall. In fact, there's a growing group who'd be content to hear a man say 'for ever', and maybe something about getting a dog.

The woman decides that a New Plan is called for. She settles on:

I'm going to be *really* sweet (to make up for the last seventeen weeks).

I guess so, but we don't have to rush in to anything, do we?

No ... it's just that the children have started to ask.

The woman gets right through the weekend without giving the man a hard time about anything. She extends her *really* sweetness to anyone who might have any influence over the man at all. (This list could include something from the animal kingdom.)

trying to impress his family

70

And she puts a fair bit of faith in some tried-and-tested techniques.

Then she has one last stab at Talking Things Over.

discussing the relationship

OH, I SEE, AND WHEN WOULD BE A GOOD TIME TO TALK ABOUT IT, ROGER?

When a woman realises that a man is displaying nine out of ten of the characteristics listed in 'Tips For Spotting Non-Committers', she has two choices. One of them is to leave him.

men leaving women

The relationship was over long before our second child was born.

A man has an off switch. Once this off switch has been pressed, a man is open to the idea of leaving a relationship. Usually he doesn't. Usually he changes his behaviour towards the woman in no way whatsoever. He just goes along. And while he is just going along, he's quite happy. This is because

71

he feels that he has been relieved of all responsibility with regard to the putting-the-relationship-on-a-firmer-footing decision. This state of affairs can last for ages. Then some nice woman from stationery supplies shows up and a few things just happen.

Often, a woman suspects that she has overstepped some sort of invisible line when she hits a man's off switch, but when the man doesn't leave her – in fact, carries on behaving pretty much as he always has – she feels reassured.

A reassured woman often favours the *really*-sweet plan. She is usually too busy with this to get suspicious until it is too late.

This sequence of events sometimes leads to women doing something fairly dramatic when the too-late part finally dawns on them.

Something to do with sugar and a petrol tank.

women leaving men

Women don't have an off switch. Women's feelings for men tend, rather, to go into a long, slow decline until they reach flatline. Once a woman's feelings have reached flatline, no amount of heart massage will revive them. A woman in flatline mode does not want to just go along. She has lots of New Plans, none of which have anything to do with the man (several of them have to do with haircuts). Quite often a woman in this frame of mind leaves a man before he has time to draw breath.

I'm sorry to have to tell you this, Colin, but lately I've grown to loathe your sunny disposition.

The flatline woman doesn't feel angry when she exits; if anything, she feels a bit sorry for the man, because she knows she is never coming back.

GOING IT ALONE

NUMBER of players: *two*
ONE MALE, *had no idea*
ONE FEMALE, *mind made up*

object
MALE: *to talk her out of it*
FEMALE: *to move on to pastures new, live a fabulous, independent life, take a long bath whenever she wants to, go to the gym regularly, eat soup for supper if she feels like it, see a lot more of her friends, take up some thrilling new hobby and meet an absolute sexpot who doesn't take her for granted*

points scored by
MALE: *for being upset but not embarrassingly distressed*
FEMALE: *for not mentioning the word 'friends'*

catchphrases
- *There's no one else*
- *I just need to do this*
- *I'll come round on Tuesday for the rest of my things*

points deducted for
MALE: *saying 'you'll never make it without me'*
FEMALE: *calling him on the first lonely Sunday after she discovers that sexpots are thin on the ground, and implying that she can't make it without him*

characteristic moves
FEMALE: *spends a long time playing solitaire*
MALE: *finds a new partner almost immediately*

The thing is, the Flatline Exit isn't the only one in the female repertoire.

We just don't get on any more.

There's the Punishment Exit and the This'll Get His Attention Exit too.

The woman knows she's making one of these because she is very, very angry with the man, and also, possibly, probably, she might come back to him if she could be sure that:

1 He would never see that slag, slapper, tramp, tart, trollopy old bimbo from stationery ever again

Why do you think that is?

2 He was prepared to put the relationship on a much firmer footing

Punishment and This'll Get His Attention Exits are reasonably successful if a man:

1 Has absolutely no desire to see what's-her-name from stationery ever again
2 Was already thinking that he probably, possibly, might put the relationship on a much firmer footing

I don't know, idiot.

The woman goes back to him four and a half minutes after one of the above has been established.

Punishment and This'll Get His Attention Exits are spectacularly unsuccessful in the following circumstances:

1 The woman from stationery's audition is going very well
2 This kind of exit, followed by reconciliation (minus the establishment of one of the above), is a regular occurrence

Exits like this come from the same behaviour school as:

issuing an ultimatum

When a woman Issues An Ultimatum she isn't necessarily packing. She just makes it very clear to a man that she is not prepared to put up with something for ever. At the end of making this clear, she gives the man a time limit. The idea is that if the man hasn't fallen into line by the time this limit is up, she will do . . . something. Like, for instance, Issue This Ultimatum again.

And this is the last time I'm going to say this.

Promise . . .

Sometimes a man is in just-going-along mode when a woman exits in order to get his attention. In circumstances like these, the man acts on reflex. He asks the woman not to go.

75

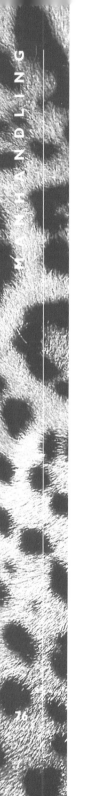

ASK AUNT LOLA
→ ADVICE FOR THE
HEARTFELT LOVELORN

Dear Aunt Lola

I've had it with putting all my energy into relationships with losers. I want a guy who acts considerate, loves me for myself, never lets me down and makes me feel like a princess.
I deserve it.

What'd you do,
doll, cure cancer?

A. L.

The woman figures she has really got his attention. She decides to milk this situation for all it is worth. She leaves, confident that she will return triumphant. Soon.

After the woman leaves, the just-going-along man switches on the telly. A rerun of an old children's science-fiction programme is on, no one is buzzing in his ear. The next day he agrees to meet the rep from the stationery suppliers.

When a man is kind of settling back into the bachelor life again (i.e. he has got a new girlfriend), he tends not to be quite so fervent with his don't-leave-me entreaties. In fact, when the woman pops round to collect some things, he makes a few distinctly casual 'Found a flat?' enquiries.

She broke off their engagement yesterday.

How awful … who's he going out with now?

The woman becomes less and less convinced re the triumphant return. She becomes more and more convinced that she's been ditched.

One night the woman is sitting up late in her new flat (small, rented). She's watching telly. A rerun of an old children's science-fiction programme comes on. She feels all sad and nostalgic (the amount of white wine that she has consumed in the course of the evening helps with this process). She decides that one more stab at Talking Things Over would be worth a shot.

The woman puts her glass down and reaches for the phone. She honestly has no intention whatsoever of giving anyone a hard time.

Ditched. Desperate. Bad.

Ditched. Desperate. Drunk. DISASTROUS.

Women forget this formula quicker than you can say: 'I can't *believe* I did that.'

Sometimes their friends help. 'Ooooh, go ahead, *call* him . . . what's the worsht he can shay?'

The kinds of calls that women make in circumstances like these always seem like a good idea at the time.

phoning him after a bit of a bust-up

A woman may not have an off switch, but she definitely has a button marked 'Self-Destruct'.

self-destructing

Every now and then a woman just goes all to pieces over a man. Ages later she will say, 'I can't *believe* I did that', but it is kind of hard to get her to see things this way at the time. At the time she thinks she might actually be able to get the man to pay some attention to her point of view, which is: 'You can't do this to me.'

Things women do in desperate attempts to get men to pay some attention to their point of view

- Make life hell for a man and his new girlfriend
- Call a man forty-five times in twenty-seven minutes (this scenario usually involves a new girlfriend too)
- Threaten lives (their own/the new girlfriend's)
- Anything to do with pregnancy

When a man is face to face with a woman who seems to have lost lots of her marbles (and a fair bit of her mascara), he is usually fairly convinced that 'doing this to her' might be the smartest move he's made for some time.

Sometimes a woman doesn't mess about with threats. Sometimes a woman gets herself a shotgun or a carving knife or a good-size car and actually has a pop at a chap.

The chap thinks this means she really loves him.

These are not the only things a woman does in the course of her love-life which make her cringe at a later date.

Things (to do with a man) that a woman has done that she feels pretty silly about now

- Leaving more than one message on a man's answering machine
- Not being able to remember exactly what she said on any of the messages
- Posting that letter
- Wearing that stupid too-tight mini dress
- Going halfway across town to some party because a man was going to be there
- Making her friend go with her to a party halfway across town that was full of drunken footballers
- Getting all dolled up and pitching up somewhere because her ex was probably going to show up
- Crying in the loo all night because her ex showed up with his new girlfriend
- Making her friend go with her
- Not going out with her friend in case a man called
- Lifting the telephone receiver to check for a dialling tone
- Answering the telephone at 11.35 p.m. and saying yes when the man who called said could he come over
- Getting all dolled up because a man was coming over at 11.35 p.m.
- Cooking elaborate meals for a man who habitually came over at 11.35 p.m.
- Believing that a man's wife didn't understand him
- Believing that a man's bank manager didn't understand him
- Believing that a man's girlfriend was very understanding
- Not realising that 'She wants to get married' meant 'I am engaged to her'
- Destroying everything a man ever gave her when she found out he was engaged (including some really nice earrings and a great silk scarf)

- Not getting out of bed for a week after this episode
- Falling for a man who was gay
- Not believing her friend when she told her the man was gay
- More or less believing the man when he told her he was gay but thinking it wouldn't hurt to spend a bit of time with him anyway
- Snogging someone at a work do
- Doing something other than snogging someone at a work do
- Snogging someone who had recently broken up with her friend
- Thinking it was cute that some guy always disconnected the phone when she came over
- Spending all that money on clothes suitable for watching motorcross in
- Buying a man a really elaborate Christmas present (breaking up with this man on the third of January)
- Crying at her birthday party because a man didn't show up
- Going to Rio because a man said 'Sure, yeah … great, why not' when she suggested following him down there in a month or two (after she'd saved all that money)
- Thinking that a man was going to propose when he took her away for a romantic weekend
- Being all mean and grumpy to a man when he was about to propose

One day you'll look back on all this and laugh.

No. One day you'll look back on all this and laugh.

A woman usually finds that her friends are only too willing to help her remember these things if she ever forgets them.

Usually when this sort of stuff is going on, there's a fair bit of Crying going on too.

ASK AUNT LOLA
ADVICE FOR THE
LOVELORN

Dear Aunt Lola

*My boyfriend got me pregnant and then he left me.
I'm devastated.*

Aunt Lola always thought that getting pregnant was
like getting your ears pierced – a
While-U-Wait procedure.

Weren't you there,
honey?

A. L.

crying

Lots of men think that women cry as a Punishment or This'll Get His Attention tactic. Mostly this is not true.

Knock, knock.

For a start, women crying is not always to do with a man . . . Women cry:

- When they are watching drama documentaries in which children are in peril
- When they are watching drama documentaries in which cute things from the animal kingdom are in peril

Who's there?

- When they are watching *Terms of Endearment* for the fifteenth time
- When their new haircut bears no resemblance whatsoever to Uma's

But sometimes it is . . .

Often, women cry and cry and cannot stop:

Boo.

- When a relationship ends

Usually, a man is in on the beginning of this process. Usually, he is not keen to see it through.

A woman's friends do this. When a relationship ends, a woman's friends come round and watch *Terms of Endearment* with her. They eat a lot of girly gooey food and they give the man a good going-over ('He's a ratbag, forget him'). The woman feels much better. Until everyone goes home. Then she starts crying and crying all over again.

. . . I don't find that funny.

One day the crying and crying stops. This is the day that the man usually picks to call the woman and see how she is.

Sometimes women cry and cry:

■ when a man is leaving town for two weeks

Some men think that the crying and crying will go on throughout this entire period. They are wrong. The woman's friends come round, they watch *Terms of Endearment*, they eat a lot of girly gooey food and they give the man a good going-over ('Listen, if he hasn't called by tomorrow, forget him'). It's a right laugh.

Quite often there is a stage before a relationship ends when a woman is very unhappy. She acts like a woman who is very unhappy. Eventually, the man says something like this to her:

> *'I think we'd better end this relationship, you're obviously very unhappy'*

and the woman plasters a grimacy grin on her face and pretends not to be unhappy at all.

A woman has to be very unhappy indeed before she gets this muddled up.

There are plenty of relationships in which hardly anyone does any crying at all. These are the relationships which are most likely to end up on a firm footing.

Where am I?

Once women are in a relationship which is on a firm footing, something they love to do is to visit a land where the sky is blue and holiday frocks abound. Men who are in relationships which have only recently got on to a firm footing usually agree to this plan with a bit more enthusiasm than they manage to muster at later dates.

The visiting-a-land-where-the-sky-is-blue-and-holiday-frocks-abound plan

You're in a five-star resort in the Indian Ocean.

Women do not make this plan because they want to watch a man windsurf.

A surprisingly large number of men seem to be in the dark about this fact.

How did I get here?

Women do not make this plan because they want to wait forty-five minutes for a man to get back from trying to track down today's newspaper.

A surprisingly large number of men seem to be in the dark about this fact.

Women do not make this plan because they want to sit idly by while a man pays a good deal of attention to what other women look like in their holiday frocks.

Most men are not in the dark about this fact for long.

I drugged you and bundled you on to a plane, dear.

A woman who is on a firm footing with a chap doesn't start crying just because his eyes wander from his newspaper towards some slapper who's strolling past in a string bikini. She gives him a playful wallop and tells him to behave. She has begun keeping him in line. Mostly, a man doesn't mind a bit.

85

STIRRING HIS STUMPS

number of players: *two*
ONE MALE, *quite happy where he is, thank you*
ONE FEMALE, *with a yen for pastures new*

object
MALE: *to relax after a hard day*
FEMALE: *to get him to agree to go somewhere*

points scored by
MALE: *for agreeing to think about it, at least*
FEMALE: *for getting a firm commitment, date and deposit out of him (for the female, 'agreeing to think about it' constitutes all of the above)*

catchphrases
■ *You'll enjoy it when you get there, you know you will*
■ *There's plenty to do*
■ *It's not that expensive*

points deducted for
MALE:
■ *refusing even to look at the brochure*
■ *saying 'foreign muck'*
FEMALE:
■ *saying 'old fart'*

characteristic moves

*FEMALE: replays her moves so many times that her opponent
    eventually becomes confused and disoriented*
MALE: checks out golf courses in the area

advanced moves

*FEMALE: if she encounters consistent resistance, may announce her
    intention to play alone or with another partner. Much is made
    of the possibilities re fun and games. This tactic sometimes
    weakens the male's defences for long enough to let the female
    slip through and book a hotel*

getting him away from it all

HERE COMES
MY SHOE
BAG

Things could go along pretty happily in the early-firm-footing-masses-of-holiday-plans stage of a relationship but for Romantic Fantasy. This is not the kind that has anything to do with fur coats and garters. It works like this.

A woman concocts an entire Romantic Fantasy starring the man in her life. In this fantasy, the man:

- Is absolutely bowled over by the sight of her in her new holiday frock
- Greets her at the station with a passionate kiss
- Says, 'Darling, this is the most delicious specially-prepared-by-your-own-fair-hands-new-recipe grilled chicken breast I have ever eaten' (or words to that effect)

The woman replays the fantasy a fair few times in her head. She gets very keen on it.

By the time she:

- Squeezes into the new holiday frock
- Steps on to the platform
- Slides the chicken on to the pre-warmed plates

Everything was wonderful at first, but then, on our honeymoon . . .

she is just filled to the brim with happy anticipation.

getting all dressed up for him

The thing is, a man is perfectly capable of looking at a woman and saying: 'You look absolutely gorgeous and that pasta was fantastic, you mean everything to me' (or words to that effect), then kissing her with lips full of love and affection. He does this on a Tuesday night after a supermarket supper in front of the telly. The woman hasn't even washed her hair. Quite often she says something like 'I haven't even washed my hair.'

It's ruined now.

But a man doesn't necessarily know his part in the holiday frock/passionate kiss/delicious new dish fantasy. The woman has been so busy rehearsing that she's forgotten to fill him in.

Tastes all right to me, love.

When the man fails miserably to pick up his cue; when the man fails miserably to follow the fantasy script, the woman is devastated.

Our marriage, you fool.

She thinks: 'Huh, I don't know why I even bother.'

She feels really angry at the man. She knows that this is a wee bit silly. She goes into a Huff.

One of a woman's favourite Romantic Fantasies involves her birthday.

A woman thinks that her birthday would be a very good time for a man to make a Romantic Gesture. (A really fabulous BIRTHDAY-sized Romantic Gesture for all the world to see.)

A man is often in the dark about this.

A woman usually forgets to fill him in.

Anyway, often a woman feels that if she does have to fill him in, if he can't figure it out for himself, then it won't be so romantic. The woman relies on the man's intuitive abilities.

Honestly, what is it with women and birthdays? You go to all this fuss and bother and then, five years later, you've got to go through it all again.

The woman figures that relying on the man's intuitive abilities might be a wee bit risky. She gives him a hint:

'Carol's husband took her to …'

She is not absolutely sure that this will do the trick. She gives him a really big hint. She makes a huge fuss on *his* birthday. Card shops are very grateful for this sequence of events.

Sometimes a woman gives a man a very difficult birthday fantasy role indeed. This typically happens on a day when a woman is feeling a bit angry, a bit unhappy, a bit flabby or a bit drab.

The man hasn't necessarily caught on to this.

Anyway, on this day, because of the above circumstances, and the fact that the woman is approaching a birthday with a number she's not keen on in it, the woman says:

'Oh, I don't know … let's not bother. It's not like it's a special birthday or anything.' (Or words to that effect.)

The man does not think this is a hint. He thinks it is a directive. He follows it.

Sometimes a really fabulous BIRTHDAY-sized Huff for all the world to see ensues.

POINTING HIM IN THE RIGHT DIRECTION

number of players: *two*
ONE MALE
ONE FEMALE, *birthday coming up*

object
MALE: *no idea*
FEMALE: *to avoid another cherry-red sweater disaster like last year's*

points scored by
MALE: *for getting the idea*
FEMALE: *for giving him the idea without resorting to removing his credit card from his pocket and handing it over*

catchphrases
■ Mmmm, that's rather nice, isn't it?
■ I prefer the black, don't you?
■ If you were stuck for an idea for my birthday . . .

points deducted for
MALE:
■ *getting the idea but thinking something similar will do*
■ *thinking something similar and cheaper will do*
■ *completely forgetting about this incident*

FEMALE:

- *not showing adequate surprise and delight if the man does remember about this incident (and where the shop was, and the size, and the colour) all by himself*
- *not showing adequate surprise and delight when the man tells her for the fifteenth time that he remembered about this incident (and where the shop was, and the size, and the colour) all by himself*

characteristic moves

FEMALE: skilfully manoeuvres the male into a suitable location for playing this game and then 'disappears for a bit' so as to give him ample opportunity to make an appropriate move. She may also use props, such as magazine pictures and advertisements, to further advance her position

MALE: knows that two routes are open to him. Taking one of them will not allow him to collect £200

G
N
I
L
D
N
A
H
N
A
M

explaining things to him

MY BIRTHDAY WAS LAST SATURDAY

A man can become rather more familiar with Huffs than he'd like.

getting in a huff

A woman finds a Huff to be a useful fallback on those occasions when she is madder at a man than his behaviour really warrants. In these circumstances the man has done something which the woman finds upsetting, but secretly, she knows that she is being a bit silly (anything to do with unfulfilled Romantic Fantasies or scheming exes tends to fall into this category).

94

Women sometimes exhibit Huff behaviour because they are suspicious about something. This something is not something about which they have any real evidence. They may have a few clues. However, these clues were gathered via means which they are not keen to divulge to the man, so they can't risk confrontation. They hope that a Huff might fluster the man and thus flush out some more information.

the if-you-don't-know-what's-wrong-I'm-not-going-to-tell-you method

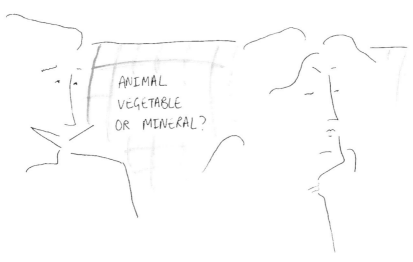

non specific huffs

What don't I understand?

Women, unlike men, sometimes just get feelings. These feelings can come over them while they are in the bath, on the motorway or fishing tea bags out of cups. These feelings don't necessarily mean anything, but they seem very important to the woman at the time. A man, because he isn't subject to this kind of thing, is not always aware of the fact that women are.

You wouldn't understand.

So, when what seems like a perfectly happy woman goes into the kitchen to make a cup of tea, and when this supposedly perfectly happy woman finds herself suddenly flooded with blue feelings and wondering if this is all life has to offer, a man doesn't necessarily catch on quick. He doesn't necessarily notice that the woman has come back into the sitting room with her blue face on and the question 'Is this all life has to offer?' in her eyes. He just says, 'Thanks, love' for his tea.

The woman is then forced to make it clear via some Huff behaviour (i.e. general restlessness, sighing, small, sad voice) that she is not happy.

A man has two responses to a Huff:

- Ignore it. This inevitably extends its length and the severity of its symptoms
- Try to fix it. Mostly, when a man tries to fix a Huff, he fails. This is because a man assumes that a Huff is always reactive. He tries to tie the woman down on exactly what is wrong. *Honestly*, if the woman knew exactly what was wrong she wouldn't be in a Huff. A bit of a barney ensues

Everything I say is wrong.

An experienced man knows that a Huff eventually responds to some old flannel and a bit of kissy-kissy. (He usually underestimates the length of time he will have to keep this up for.) So he acts all affectionate to the woman when she is talking on the phone to her mother.

What a silly thing to say.

When a woman has been coming home on a regular basis, for a fair old while, to a man who loves her enough to weather the odd Huff, she tends to forget the efforts she made in the past to ensure that this would happen one day.

The efforts a woman made in the past to ensure that this would happen one day

- 'Wear that holiday thing you've got'
- 'You *have* to read this book'
- 'Yes, I think we have a thirty-four B in red'
- 'You just put a flowering plant in the south-west corner of your bedroom and . . . bingo'
- 'Don't call him'
- 'You're going to look *just* like Uma'

It's not that she stops making any effort for him.

It's just that her efforts develop a special-occasion flavour.

In between special occasions, a woman realises that the man, lovable as he is, has his faults. That he is, after all, *just* a man and that there are quite a few things that *she* has to put up with.

Things up with which a woman puts, in order to have a man in her life

- Having to cook for someone who doesn't think a baked potato constitutes a meal
- Having someone cook for her who creates a small mountain of used cooking utensils in the process
- Having to explain why the heroine is crying when they're watching something subtle on the telly
- Having to explain why *she* is crying when they're watching something subtle on the telly
- Having to repeat herself even if nobody is crying
- Having to explain who is married to whom on the way home in the car after dinner parties
- Having to drive home after dinner parties
- Having to buy the postcards
- Having to write the postcards

- Having to wait for things to get fixed because: (a) it's man's work; (b) it's a waste of money to get *another* man in; (c) he's *SAID* he'll do it, *OK?*
- Having to get a man in after he's fixed things
- Laundry
- The whole wet towel business
- Quite a lot of other things to do with the bathroom
- Hearing someone shout obscenities at the television set during sports programmes
- Sports programmes
- Incidents to do with four extra people and lunch/supper/accommodation for the weekend
- Having someone say 'Don't make a fuss' during the four extra people and lunch/supper/accommodation for the weekend incident
- Having to sleep in a room with a Siberian draught blowing through it
- Having to sleep in a room with someone who is snoring (this can be a deal-breaker)

All right, let's compromise. You never cut your toenails on the bed again and I'll let you live.

One more thing . . .

- the male ego

massaging his ego

Most women consider a man's ego to be a fragile thing. Sometimes they flatter a fellow just to keep him happy. Sometimes they keep their traps shut when a chap is pointing out some of his amazing abilities to them.

tolerating his taste in décor

CAUGHT BY J.T.THOMPSON

Women can't keep this up for ever. They have to go into the kitchen and roll their eyes every now and again.

Luckily, a man is usually a bit busy feeling important to notice when this happens.

Massaging His Ego has a cousin: Letting Him Win. Modern women might give this a whirl in the Absolute Adoration stage. But mostly, they can't resist seeing the look on a man's face when he's been absolutely thrashed at something by a girl.

Of course, men could make a very long women-list like this. Most of them would start it with a sentence that had the word 'talking' in it. There is something, though, that women tend to do a bit more of than men in the putting-up with line.

It's this:

taking up the slack

If a man behaves badly in public a woman often feels that it's her job to make up for it.

This means that a man who is rude to waiters very often has a woman at his side who is grinning inanely and making pathetic attempts to ingratiate herself with the entire restaurant staff.

The grinning-inanely-and-making-pathetic-attempts-to-ingratiate-herself method, example two

A couple are having dinner at someone's house. The hostess's husband is an idiot with halitosis.

The male half of the couple assumes an expression which reads 'You're an idiot with halitosis' and proceeds to withdraw pretty much entirely from the normal social proceedings.

The female half of the couple spots this development from two hundred paces, and proceeds to grin inanely. She tries to draw her man back into the normal social proceedings. She says 'we' a lot, as in 'Don't we . . .?', in a pathetic attempt to make this happen. She is awfully sweet to the idiot with halitosis.

'My husband didn't mean to offend you. It's just that he doesn't suffer fools gladly.'

ASK AUNT LOLA
ADVICE FOR THE
LOVELORN

Dear Aunt Lola

My husband is a doctor. All he does is work, work, work. I never see him. I'm fed up with it.

Was he a doctor when you married him?

Didn't you notice?

A. L

On the way home in the car, when the man says, 'I can't believe you spent all evening gassing to that idiot with halitosis', a woman often wishes that she hadn't. Because, secretly, the woman really, really wishes she could be more like the man. But she can't.

Some men think that modern women want to *be* men. They are wrong. Modern women covet men's ability not to care about so many things (waiters' feelings, soft furnishings, appropriate shoes). They wish they could sail through birthdays with four in them the way that men can. But the penis envy theory is codswallop.

What women really envy is being able to pee standing up, outdoors, pretty much anywhere, without a passing thought for the well-being of a skirt hem.

Still, men do not get to chat when they pee. In fact they don't get to chat to each other all that much when they're doing anything. This means they rarely achieve the level of gender solidarity that women do when it comes to dealing with the opposite sex.

The up-with-which-I-have-to-put list makes excellent conversation fodder for women. Generally, women prefer this conversation to the what-he-meant-by-soon one. They can keep it up for an age. All this chatting affects the man because the women pool information. Some of this information is negative: 'He's having an affair.' Some of it is positive: 'He took me to . . .' Either way a woman gets to thinking. She thinks, 'If *her* husband can do it . . .'

They're all just big kids, aren't they?

In negative information circumstances a woman begins to worry about her own man's potential with regard to the type of behaviour described.

No, mine's an old goat.

She can't ignore the wee bit of suspiciousness that wells up inside her. She decides that some casual scrutiny might not be a silly idea.

If this casual scrutiny turns up anything like a matchbook from a restaurant she can't remember ever eating at, the man finds himself on the receiving end of either a Huff or a whopping great tropical mosquito of an interrogation. Sometimes, in a very firm-footing situation, a woman doesn't bother beating about the bush. She just Lets The Man Have It.

letting him have it

'I told him he was a pig-ugly, useless, bone-idle, space-wasting, lying snake in the grass with breath like a sewer and bananas for brains ... and then I said something I regret.'

A woman Lets A Man Have It when she is absolutely one hundred per cent convinced (and then some) that he is absolutely one hundred per cent (and then some) In The Wrong.

A man who is absolutely one hundred per cent In The Wrong usually knows it. He tries a few half-hearted deflecting tactics, but then he takes his telling-off on the chin.

Sometimes a woman gets a bit drunk with power at this stage and throws in a few other things that the man has done which are in the ... well, OK, about sixty-per-cent-In-The-Wrong category. She loses her advantage.

Sometimes a man reacts to a confrontational telling-off with an explanation. When this happens, a woman is *forced* to resort to the sixty-per-cent category so as to save herself from looking a wee bit silly.

GANGING UP ON HIM

number of players: *any number*
ONE MALE, *not a hundred per cent comfortable*
MORE THAN ONE FEMALE, *laughing*

object
MALE: *to hold on to his pride*
FEMALES: *to make the man aware that he is a member of a cute but inferior species*

points scored by
MALE: *for taking it all in good part*
FEMALES: *for making a man laugh while he's getting a right going-over*

catchphrases
- *Hopeless*
- *Keep up*
- *MEN!!*

points deducted for
MALE:
- *sulking*
- *telling a joke which begins 'No one would talk to women if they didn't have . . .'*

FEMALES:

- *meanness*
- *telling a joke which begins 'What do you call a man with half a brain?'*

characteristic moves

FEMALES: disarm the male by stroking, squeezing and petting him at frequent intervals and maintaining a jocular, teasing stance throughout the cut-and-thrust

MALE: cannot win. Once a male is experienced enough to accept this, he usually finds the game quite enjoyable

Women have a tendency to increase the odds that they will look a wee bit silly by convincing themselves of a man's In The Wrongness via some fairly flimsy evidence.

Examples of fairly flimsy evidence

- A programme on the telly about handwriting analysis which said that people who write their Y's like him are always unfaithful
- Something which looks like the back of an earring which all the women who've been in this car say does not belong to them
- 'I *called* the office . . .'

The thing is that in the shaky-footing days of relationships a man's In The Wrongness pretty much stops there. Once a relationship is on rock-solid ground, though, a man's In the Wrongness potential expands a bit. Very few men are in the dark about this fact.

An example of an In The Wrong situation which tends to arise once a relationship is on rock-solid ground:

'Carol's husband took her to . . .' (somewhere that the woman has been mentioning incessantly for about three months). A man is often pretty adept at ignoring comments like this from the woman he lives with. (The amount of time he has been living with her often has a direct bearing on this situation.) So, sometimes another woman intervenes on her behalf. This woman could be a friend, family member, work colleague or a complete stranger who was standing in the lingerie section of a department store on the last shopping day before Christmas.

Things (to do with a man) that a woman has done for another woman

- Explained to a man about women and flowers
- Ordered the flowers
- Reminded a man that it is a woman's birthday
- Made a few suggestions to a man with regard to suitable presents
- Helped a man to purchase suitable presents
- Valentine's Day (ditto)
- Mother's Day (ditto)
- Made it clear to a man that she knows what he's up to
- Suggested that a man buy an engagement ring
- Helped a man pick out an engagement ring
- Reminded a man to take good care of a woman who is pregnant
- Suggested that a man buy an eternity ring for a woman who has had a baby
- Told a man that the black would be more useful
- Let a man 'see something on' (despite men's high hopes and big talk this is more likely to involve a sales assistant and a scarf than a complete stranger and lingerie)

Hello, Miss Smith, I want to thank you for the lovely flowers my husband sent me.

There's another thing that women do for other women (to do with men): Set Them Up. In this scenario a man who was planning a nice night in with a few sports programmes is badgered into coming to supper by the wife of a friend. At this supper he is seated next to a woman who spends the entire evening staring at the floor and muttering something about a boyfriend in Australia.

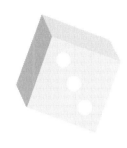

SETTING HIM UP

number of players: *three*
ONE MALE, eligible
TWO FEMALES, one scheming, one resigned

object
MALE: to get a drink
FEMALES: one, to brighten the lives of two lonely people; two, to make a last, probably hopeless, attempt to convince herself that there is a male out there who is halfway decent-looking, heterosexual, intelligent, interesting, employed, honest, funny and single (employed is optional)

points scored by
MALE: for living up to the glowing reports given about him by one of the females to the other
FEMALES: one, for producing a male who is halfway decent-looking, heterosexual, intelligent, interesting, employed, honest, funny and single; two, for showing up

catchphrases
- What have you got to lose?
- It won't be like a set-up
- So how's it going, you two?

points deducted for

MALE:

■ *bringing a date*

FEMALE ONE:

■ *producing a geek*

■ *making it very difficult for Female Two to escape the geek*

FEMALE TWO:

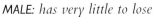 *making an unacceptably early and obvious escape from the geek*

characteristic moves

FEMALES: spend a great deal of time prior to and during the game discussing strategies. This is done with lots more enthusiasm on the part of Female One than Female Two, unless Female One's ploys are successful. In which case, Female Two becomes the spearhead whilst Female One operates in an advisory capacity

MALE: has very little to lose

There are some things up with which a woman will not put.

These are things which warrant something more serious than a Huff and something more dignified than a confrontation ('I don't even want to discuss it'). A man usually knows what they are.

When a man is about to step into the doghouse he usually has a fleeting thought which goes a bit like this:

'I'm really going to be in the doghouse now.'

He ignores it. Very, very, very much later, when he sees the woman he loves looking very unhappy indeed, he is, sometimes, just a wee bit genuinely repentant. It's no good. The woman is giving him the Cold Shoulder.

giving him the cold shoulder

Cold Shoulder tactics

She hasn't spoken to me for a week.

- Not speaking, at all, for ages
- Speaking in teeny, tiny clipped little sentences after not speaking, at all, for ages
- Making it very clear that no physical contact will be welcomed
- Being very stiff and unwelcoming when the man makes a foolish attempt at physical contact
- Not answering the telephone
  - Getting a little thrill of triumph when the telephone rings for ages
  - Having frequent mental dialogues which go like this: 'I'd be so much happier with a nice little flat and a cat'

It's hard to find a woman like that.

A wee-bit-genuinely-repentant man usually responds to a Cold Shoulder with some old flannel – 'I would have called but I thought you'd be asleep' – and a bit of a kissy-kissy. (A woman usually overestimates the amount of time that a man is prepared to keep this up for.) It is not unknown for a woman to allow a Cold Shoulder to take over her whole body for what seems like an Ice Age to a man. In circumstances like these, a man usually goes out and gets himself into the sort of trouble that warrants this type of response.

There are some things that a woman doesn't want to put up with. These things are not in the Cold Shoulder league. They don't even warrant Huffs, although a woman forgets this from time to time. They are just teeny, tiny things (to do with the man) that the woman thinks she'd be happier without. She sets about changing them.

changing a man

In extreme cases a woman takes on a known rogue and then spends a great deal of time whining, wheedling, pleading and cajoling with him to give up the habits of a lifetime for her sake, not to mention the kids' (who she mentions incessantly). The whining, wheedling pleading and cajoling does have some effect. The man gives up the habits of a lifetime for approximately four and a half minutes. This length of time decreases as the relationship progresses.

I don't want you to do it because I want you to do it. I want you to want to do it.

How many girlfriends does it take to change a lightbulb? ...Just one, but the lightbulb has to want to change ...

Ha ...ha.

111

Mostly, though, a woman takes on a fairly average sort of Joe and just has a go at Polishing Him Up A Bit.

Polishing-Him-Up-A-Bit methods:

- Suggesting that he changes his jacket.
- Buying him a nice new jacket for his birthday

A woman who sets about trying to change a man too vigorously lays herself open to charges of Nagging.

nagging

Nagging is a word that men use when women ask them things more than once.

'How many times have I asked you not to do that?'

Men do not think that they play any part in the fact that women ask them things more than once.

'Uh-huh . . .'

Men do not think that *they* are Nagging when they say, 'If you don't *reverse* it in you'll *never* get it out' for the fourteenth time this month.

Anyway, often a woman is not Nagging. She is simply looking after a fellow's better interests.

Some men moan about women trying to change them. They say they wish women would love them just as they are.

Not very many men who would like women to love them just as they are would like the women in their lives to stop shaving their armpits.

'I thought you were counting.'

One of the things that encourages a woman with regard to the Changing A Man policy is the fact that often he doesn't put up too much resistance.

ASK AUNT LOLA
ADVICE FOR THE
LOVELORN

Dear Aunt Lola

I've met a man who has a few problems with drink, and the police sometimes give him a hard time, but he is a real sweetie and I am going to move in with him. My friends say I'm crazy. What do you think?

Is there a small winged creature perched on your shoulder whispering, 'You can help this man' into your ear?

KILL IT.

A. L

*Anything to eat?
Seen my keys?
What's the
number?*

Once a man is comfortable in a relationship with a woman, there is usually a fair old chunk of his life which he is quite happy for her to be in charge of.

At first the woman willingly takes responsibility for birthdays, gas bills, vitamins, the bathroom, keys, remembering where he left his briefcase and making social arrangements. She takes control with regard to washing and soft furnishings as well, but she leaves taxes and motor mechanics to him. For a while everything goes along quite smoothly. But then the woman starts to feel edgy. Sometimes this edginess is exacerbated by the sight of her beloved staring blankly at a restaurant menu and asking, 'What do I like?'

*Want a
divorce?*

Some women just sigh and settle in and start behaving like the man's mother at this stage. They say, 'Who do you think I am, your mother?' an awful lot. This enquiry always makes men uncomfortable.

Other enquiries that make men uncomfortable

- 'Which one do *you* like?'
- 'What shall I wear?'
- 'What time will you be back?'
- 'What's *that*?'

'Who do you think I am, your mother?' has a variant: 'Who do you think I am, your housekeeper?' Either way, a man would not like to be forced into giving the woman he lives with an honest answer. He doesn't have to. When a man says a sentence which starts with the words 'Where are my . . .' a woman feels irritated. Often, she acts irritated. But deep, deep in the darkest corner of her psyche, a little voice starts up.

This is what it says:

'It really is your job, you know.
You're the woman …'

Are you
employed full
time?

Yes.
I'm a woman.

Little voices say this kind of thing to women
who are running major multinationals.

Things that even the most modern woman has done for a man rather more often than he has done them for her

- Sewn on a button
- Made a hot lemon drink
- Ironed a shirt
- Taken clothing from the back of a chair and put it on a hanger
- Taken something to the dry-cleaner's
- Rolled socks into pairs
- Straightened a tie
- Brushed lint from a jacket
- Found the aspirins
- Bought razor blades
- Washed underwear
- Run a bath
- Posted a birthday card
- Stuck a plaster on
- Made breakfast
- Made a bed
- Made an appointment
- Picked out a book
- Picked something up off the floor
- Schlepped to some specialist store halfway across town to buy something related to a hobby

I got some
new socks for
my husband.

Good trade.

helping him to shoulder his responsibilities

IF SHE DOESN'T MAKE ME GET UP SOON I'LL BE LATE

When the woman hears the little voice she feels even more irritated. She acts even more irritated. She gets out of bed, opens a drawer and flings a pair of socks in a man's general direction.

Some women get pretty darned good at ignoring the little voice.

Little voices aren't so easily put off:

'Somewhere out there lives a lovely young thing, with hair just like Uma's, who would go to a man's office wearing fur coats and garters on a regular basis, and never get irritated.'

Often a modern woman tries to overcome the mother/housekeeper/little voice problem by encouraging the man to see their relationship as a partnership. One day she gets him to come to the supermarket with her. She asks him if he would prefer tagliatelle or spaghetti. The man doesn't give a tossed salad.

The woman picks up on this pretty quick. The woman thinks: 'Why do I have to do *everything*?'

A Huff is fairly evident in the car on the way home.

Sometimes a woman who is encouraging a man to see their relationship as a partnership skips the supermarket part. She thinks it would be a good idea for them to do more fun things together. She asks the man to teach her how to windsurf. She is absolutely stunned at the speed with which her erstwhile equal partner turns into the sergeant major from hell.

It's like this.

- A man likes someone to be in charge
- A man thinks that when the woman is in charge she ought to just get on with it and not bother him
- A man figures that a woman who asks for his help is asking *him* to take charge

'I said, keep your arms straight!'

joining in with his leisure pursuits

YOU'RE OBVIOUSLY NOT PREPARED TO TAKE THIS SERIOUSLY

Wheeee

Eventually, women who've managed to get a man to come round to their way of thinking on a few things . . .

improving his dress sense

and have come round to his way of thinking on a few others . . .

bowing to his superior knowledge

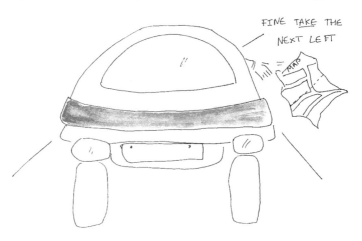

FINE TAKE THE NEXT LEFT

give up on trying to make fundamental changes.

These women no longer expect men to sit around on sun loungers and chat. They've noticed that most of them seem more content when they're intent on something.

'I think if I go over to the next village I'll find they've got The Times.'

A woman like this *encourages* a man to keep busy. If he hasn't thought of a project for himself, she thinks of one for him.

finding him a project

In the modern relationship, this doesn't necessarily have anything to do with shelves.

Things a woman has asked a man to do

- Hang a picture
- Clean windows
- Change a lightbulb
- Change a tap washer
- Wash a car
- The lawn
- Her taxes
- Deal with the man who has come round to do one of the above
- Negotiate the price of something
- Lift something
- Carry something
- Assemble something that comes in an impossible-to-assemble kit (rolled her eyes a wee bit when the man pointed this out to her)
- Light a fire

119

- Fix a drink
- Open a jar
- Go to the bar to buy the drinks
- Go downstairs in the middle of the night
- Carve meat
- Take the rubbish out
- Take the dog out
- Build something
- Barbecue something
- Go round the supermarket with a list
- Select the wine in the supermarket while she goes round with a list

A man does most of these things fairly happily, but a woman always suspects that he would do them with real enthusiasm if he were asked by a pretty nurse.

A woman who's been on a firm footing with a man for a while is also reasonably encouraging with regard to hobbies. This encouragement tends to backfire occasionally – 'It's my *birthday*' – but still, it does make present-buying much easier.

There's another reason why a woman likes it if a man has something to do. It's this.

When a man loves a woman, he often wants rather a lot of her attention. A woman tends to fall in with this desire readily during the heady Absolute Adoration days, but the thing is, now, though of course she still adores the man, it's just that . . . Sometimes, she's busy.

Sometimes, she fancies a bit of time to herself.

Sometimes, the thrill of seeing someone windsurf has just plain worn off.

being impressed by his fabulous feats of daring

A man hasn't necessarily kept abreast of these developments. Sometimes he is just a wee bit . . . hurt by them. Sometimes he thinks something like this to himself:

'She obviously doesn't care about me at all.'

He goes into a bit of a Huff.

GIVING HIM STRICT INSTRUCTIONS

number of players: *two*
ONE MALE, *bit busy*
ONE FEMALE, *busier*

object
MALE: *a quiet life*
FEMALE: *to get a man to make himself useful*

points scored by
MALE: *for making himself useful, in a willing and cheerful manner*
FEMALE: *for having complete faith that the man will make himself useful in a willing and cheerful manner*

catchphrases
■ *But I specifically asked you …*
■ *How could you forget?*
■ *Oh, don't bother, I'll do it myself*

points deducted for
MALE:
■ *not remembering what he was specifically asked*
■ *remembering what he was specifically asked but not remembering to do it*
■ *letting her do it herself*

FEMALE:

- *doing it herself in an extremely unwilling and cheerless manner*
- *making sure the man remembers that this happened*

Characteristic moves

FEMALE: takes to repeating all instructions, several times, in child's-play language

MALE: plays dead

being sensitive to his moods

The woman notices that the man is in a bit of a Huff. She thinks about the days when she used to run around after him like a silly bit of a kid. She thinks about how much happier she is now.

The woman gives the man some old flannel.

The man figures he's really got her attention now. He milks this situation for all it is worth.

The woman gives the man a bit of kissy-kissy.

Before you can say Canary, the man is happily chattering about all his adventures.

listening attentively to his tales from the battle front

And they make up.

comforting him in his hour of need

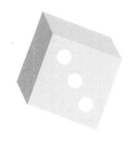

LIVING HAPPILY EVER AFTER

number of players: *two*
ONE MALE
ONE FEMALE

object
MALE: to keep things exactly as they are
FEMALE: to change pretty much everything, starting with the
   curtains

points scored by
MALE: for meeting her halfway
FEMALE: for meeting him halfway

catchphrases
■ *Why would you want to keep that?*
■ *We're giving up beef*
■ *What do you think of mauve for that back bedroom?*

points deducted for

MALE:

- *being a stick-in-the-mud*
- *saying 'ask the boss'*

FEMALE:

- *skipping even the most notional attempts at consultation*
- *saying 'oh, don't mind him'*

characteristic moves

FEMALE: does her best to convince the male that every move she makes is an advancement for both of them

MALE: plays along most of the time and only puts a marker down on big issues (like giving up his school cricket sweater)

ASK AUNT LOLA
ADVICE FOR THE
LOVELORN

Dear Aunt Lola

I want to say something to all those griping gals out there. Quit looking for Prince Charming, settle for a decent guy. He might have his faults but what's a little snoring if you get to wake up every day next to someone who cares?

You tell 'em, sugar. No point skipping breakfast just 'cos there's butter in the jelly.

A. L.